ALONG THE WAY

ALONG THE WAY

Trudy Cathy White

Published by Looking Glass Books
Decatur, Georgia

Manufactured in the United States of America
ISBN 1-929619-21-9

Scripture quotations are from:
The Holy Bible: New Living Translation
Copyright © 1996 by Tyndale
HousePublishers, Inc.

ALONG THE WAY

ACKNOWLEDGEMENTS

A special thanks goes to Kara Gallagher, who has made this project a reality. She spent endless hours helping me compile some of my life stories. It was my joy to know her while living in Richmond, Virginia. Kara is a former elementary school teacher and spent three years in Maribor, Slovenia, as a journeyman with the International Mission Board.

I am forever grateful to my husband, John, who has encouraged me to write *Along the Way*. Ever since we were married in 1977, he has been my faithful companion and prayer partner. His deep commitment to the Lord and love for me has motivated and inspired me to fulfill God's purposes in my life.

Last, but certainly not least, I want to express thanks to my wonderful children who have offered so much support to me throughout the years. Parenting is such a rewarding opportunity from God. What a joy to know each of our children take such a strong stand for their Lord. We have truly been blessed with Trent (son-in-law) and Joy, John IV, and Kylie (daughter-in-law), Angela, and David.

To my parents, two brothers, and their wives, nieces and nephews, in-laws and extended family— I love you all

DEDICATION

*She is clothed with strength and dignity, and
she laughs with no fear of the future. When
she speaks, her words are wise, and kindness
is the rule when she gives instructions.
She carefully watches all that goes on in her
household and does not have to bear the
consequences of laziness. Her children will
stand and bless her. Her husband praises her:
"There are many virtuous and capable women in
the world, but you surpass them all!"*
—*Proverbs 31:25-29*

This book is dedicated to my mother, Jeannette
McNeil Cathy—my lifelong inspiration. Though I
am now a mother myself with grown children, she
still takes time to call and offer me encouragement
from God's Word. I cherish each moment when
she calls and takes the time to listen and share her
godly wisdom.

Among Mother's many talents is the gift of being an artist. Like most artists, she places her initials on her painting—claiming the work as her own
before the world. In a real sense I, too, am a prod-
uct of her art because of the powerful truths about

God that she modeled and taught throughout my formative years.

I can only hope that as a result of her early and lasting efforts, God's "initials"can be clearly seen in me. Mother raised three children who are committed to the Lord, and we gladly stand and bless her. She is a blessing to her grandchildren by her dedication to daily prayer for each of them. Yes, she is still working on her masterpiece to the glory of the Father.

Mother: I'm forever grateful for your love and guidance all along the way.

Your daughter,
Trudy Cathy White

ALONG THE WAY

LOST BUT FOUND

Show me the path where I should walk, O LORD;
point out the right road for me to follow.
—Psalm 25:4

Have you ever thought about how many ways there are to be lost? You can be lost in terms of location. Finding yourself lost in an unfamiliar area of a city or inside an enormous building is not fun. You can also be lost when trying to learn something new or when listening to someone tell a story. This kind of lostness deals with a lack of understanding, and you might say, "I'm completely lost when it comes to calculus," or "You totally lost me on that one." I've even heard it said that you can be lost for words, though I've never experienced that situation personally! Seriously though, one way that all of us are lost is spiritually. Without Jesus Christ in your life, your spirit, which is made to live forever, will be lost to an eternity in hell . . .

In 1962, at the age of seven, I understood that God loved me. I learned from the Bible that God loved me so much, He sent His Son, Jesus, to die on the cross. Jesus died to pay the penalty for the sins I committed against Him.

My parents, along with my pastor and Sunday school teachers, also taught me that God wants everyone to go to heaven when he or she dies. The only way to heaven is to accept God's gift of love, His Son, Jesus. Jesus died in my place. I didn't have to think too long to realize that what I had heard about God was the truth, and I wanted to accept His love.

One afternoon after school, my pastor, Brother Brown, came by our house and, with my parents by my side, I prayed, asking Jesus to take control of my life. I admitted that I needed His forgiveness, as I had already developed a bad habit of lying, and I very much wanted to go to heaven one day. At such a young age, I could not possibly realize how this single decision would radically change the course of my life forever, but I knew that I was no longer lost.

Years later, in 1973, that assurance was tested in Paris, France. It was my first time to visit Paris, and while wandering about the city alone, I suddenly realized that I did not know my way back to the hotel. My emotions began to escalate, and I felt everything from loneliness and confusion to downright hopelessness. Dusk fell, and as darkness slowly enveloped the city, I looked around with the understanding that no one could help me. I thought, *I'll never find my way back.* I was totally out of solutions, ideas, energy, and hope. With no idea of where to turn and no hunch about what to do, I sat down a bit dejectedly on a bench at the crossroads of the city's major arteries.

I was convinced that bench was a "safe" place for me, as it was the only place that looked even remotely familiar. Then I cried out in my heart to God, "If I'm ever going to find my way back, You will have to show me the way. I'm not going to look any longer." With that, God gave me the greatest gift ever—the assurance of His presence, right there on a bench in the middle of Paris! Because I knew He was with me, my loneliness diminished; because I knew He was in control, my despair vanished; because I knew He loved me, my confusion began to lift. Almost the instant I acknowledged my complete dependence upon Him, I heard one of my traveling companions call out from across the street, "Trudy, what are you doing over there?"

Have you heard God calling you? You probably haven't heard an audible voice like the voice of my friend, but He is calling you just the same. God wants you to know that you don't have to be lost any longer either! So, if you're sitting on one of life's benches, weary from the ups and down of everyday life, lonely, confused, and wrapped in darkness, just answer His call.

Perhaps you have known the joy of the Lord for a long time. Are you lighting the way for others to respond to His voice? As followers of Jesus, we are responsible for sharing God's love with all who still are lost.

In 1984, after having been in Brazil for just two weeks, I was driving home with the children. Unexpectedly, the car just stopped running. With tears in her eyes and fear on her face, Joy said, "But Mommy, we can't even speak Portuguese!" That much I already knew without her reminding me. God used that situation to help me comfort Joy and John-John as I shared with them that God would protect us and give us wisdom about what to do. Can you imagine if I had just ignored their distress and had gone about the business of trying to find a solution to my problem? Imagine if I had just moved on without addressing those tears and the fear growing in my children's hearts. What kind of mother would I have been to act so callously?

What kind of Christian ignores the cries of the lost all around him? What kind of Christian goes about her daily life without addressing the most urgent need of those around her—the need for a saving knowledge of Jesus Christ? The next time God leads you to share with a lost person, what will you do?

What about you?

Describe a time when you lost something important to you, a time when you felt lost while someone was explaining a new concept to you, or a time when you were lost in a city or building. Imagine for a moment being lost forever. If what Jesus said was true, what do you have to lose by following Him?

HE'S ALWAYS THERE

"For the mountains may depart and the hills disappear,
but even then I will remain loyal to you. My
covenant of blessing will never be broken,"
says the LORD, who has mercy on you.
—Isaiah 54:10

We are so accustomed to the saying "Seeing is be-lieving" that often we don't stop to think about how many things we do not see and yet choose to believe. For example, I've never seen the gold in Fort Knox, but when someone gives me a five-dollar bill, I believe that rectangular piece of paper is actually worth something. I've never seen my liver, but I live each day with the knowledge that it must be there, working away. Imagine how silly I would look if I claimed, "Liver? What liver? I've never seen my liver, so I must not have one!" When I was a girl, I had a meaningful experience that taught me about the presence of God in my life. I might not see God or even sense His closeness at times, but I can always be certain that He's there, working away . . .

Every summer, from the time I was seven years old until I was seventeen, my parents let me attend a session at Camp Crestridge for Girls in the mountains of North Carolina. During each session about one hundred girls gathered to stay in the rustic cabins, swim in the mountain lake, and learn more about our Savior and ourselves. Going to Camp Crestridge was a good experience for me, and I carried away from it some lifelong memories, friends, and lessons.

My second or third summer at camp, when I was about nine, I learned a lesson that has always been dear to my heart. Each week all of us gathered around a big campfire for a time of worship and reflection. On those evenings around twilight, a bell rang, abruptly ending the conversations taking place on each rolling hill and in every cabin throughout the camp. It was the call to the campfire! Grabbing sweatshirts to ward off the cool mountain air, we set off for the campfire without a word. Immediately, the vacuum left by the end of our conversations became filled with the squeaking of spring-hinged doors and subsequent slams as we exited our cabins. The sweet smell of burning wood enveloped us, hanging in the summer air as a reminder of the cookout we had enjoyed earlier around our cabins. As our little army of campers made its way down the hillsides, the rhythmic crunch of gravel resounded amidst the gurgling of the stream that fed our lake. The crickets were just gearing up for their nightly serenade, and up ahead we could hear the sound of recorded singing coming from the sound system. As we drew closer, the snap and sizzle of the bonfire rounded out the familiar sounds of those evenings.

One night after we had all gathered and situated ourselves on the wooden benches around the fire, overlooking the lake and majestic mountains on the far side, our camp assistant, Johnnie Armstrong, stood to speak. She called to our attention that the mountains around us were completely invisible due to low clouds. Looking out, I could see that indeed, the rolling peaks had been obscured. Then Johnnie asked a simple but profound question: "Even though you can't see the mountains, how many of you believe they're still there? Raise your hand if you are certain."

That was a defining moment for me. I raised my hand with the utmost confidence; I believed! There was no doubt in my mind. Those mountains were definitely still there. Is there anything more sincere than the innocent, complete certainty we experience in childhood? Then Johnnie drove her point home. She said, "There will be times in your life when you will ask yourself, 'Has God abandoned me? Has He turned His back on me? Is He still here?' You can be as sure of His presence and love as you are right now about the presence of those mountains."

In those moments, the assurance that God would never leave me or forsake me, that He would be with me wherever I went, was born in my heart.

What about you?

Have you ever experienced a moment when you realized a great truth that made you feel like you were walking on air for a day or two or maybe longer? Describe that moment and the impact it has had on your life. If you haven't experienced one of these "eureka" moments, take a moment to ponder the significance of the scripture at the beginning of this devotion. If you could be assured of the truth of this verse, how would such knowledge change your way of thinking about life?

JUST A PENNY

*Unless you are faithful in small matters, you won't
be faithful in large ones. If you cheat even a little,
you won't be honest with greater responsibilities.*
—*Luke 16:10*

Often the most memorable lessons are learned at
the greatest price. Looking back at this incident, the
cost of my lesson doesn't seem too great, though it
seemed devastating at the time . . .

Each week my mother drove my brother Dan and
me to piano lessons with Mr. Edwards in East Point,
Georgia. I had my lesson first while Dan sat in the car
with Mother, doing his homework. As always, Mother
never wasted a moment to idleness; she used this time
to prepare for teaching her Sunday school class.

One afternoon, as I finished my lesson, Mr. Edwards
was talking with Dan as I headed out to join Mother in
the car. As I gathered my music books to leave, I happened to notice a penny sitting on the corner of Mr.
Edwards's coffee table. Without a second thought, I

picked it up and skipped down the front steps to the car. I opened the door and sat beside Mother. As I prepared to begin my homework, I admired the penny in my hand and rolled it around a bit. For some reason, that attracted Mother's attention and she asked, "Trudy, where did you get that penny?" Her question sparked the first uncomfortable stirrings that perhaps I had done something wrong by taking the penny. Guilt bubbled up in my heart as I haltingly replied, "Well, I just picked it up off Mr. Edwards's coffee table." To my utter dismay, she said, "You need to take that penny back to him. It's not yours." I responded to this shocking statement, "But Mom, it's just a penny! He won't even miss it. He probably didn't even know it was there to begin with. Besides, you can't really do much with a penny."

But my rationalization did nothing to convince Mother. She explained how wrong that thinking was. "You can't take things that don't belong to you," she said. "The Bible calls that stealing." She looked me squarely in the eyes and said, "Trudy, you will take that penny back to Mr. Edwards, and you are going to apologize to him and admit your wrong." At that pronouncement, I threw a rather unlovely fit and insisted that there was no way I could possibly carry out such a request. Mother calmly said, "We are not leaving until you take care of this. You may wait until Dan's lesson is finished, but you *will* do as I have asked."

After an agonizing half hour, I did end up going back, though it was tremendously difficult for me to walk up those steps and face Mr. Edwards. As I recall, I felt horrible about having picked up that penny, but for some reason the fact I had done something wrong did not register with me yet—it was just a penny. When I told Mr. Edwards what I had done and handed the penny to him, I felt even more terrible. I was eager to get back in the car and leave the whole matter behind me.

Interestingly enough, I have never really left it behind. That experience profoundly affected me. To this day if I see a penny somewhere, perhaps in a parking lot, I don't dare pick it up because it's not mine. I learned a lasting life lesson: not to bother other people's things and not to take what doesn't belong to me without asking. That painful experience taught me a very healthy lesson: be honest when dealing with others' possessions. You see, it wasn't a matter of just a penny after all.

What about you?

Think back to a lesson you learned as a child. Describe the circumstances surrounding the lesson, including the people involved, the words said, and your feelings at the time. What impact has this lesson had on your life?

HIS PLAN

Love the LORD your God, walk in all his ways,
obey his commands, be faithful to him, and
serve him with all your heart and all your soul.
—*Joshua 22:5*

By nature, most of us are planners. The market today for Palm Pilots, Day-Timers, calendars, and other products that help us plan and organize our time is a veritable gold mine. We plan where we will go to school; then we plan our academic schedule. We plan where to work and where to live, when to get married and when to have children. We plan vacations and where and how we'll spend retirement. We like to have a plan.

Surprises can be nice, as long as they don't interfere too drastically with "the plan." Christians are called to place their plans under the lordship of Jesus Christ. Sometimes this may mean letting go of them all together . . .

When I was a teenager, I often thought about missionaries and daydreamed about what their lives must be like. Serving God in faraway places, experiencing the wonders of an exotic culture, and learning a new language sounded so intriguing to me. My youthful heart was open to such an adventure. I could envision myself serving the Lord in some foreign land, but I never let myself dwell too seriously on the subject. After all, I was too young to be considering any definite plans.

In high school, at Woodward Academy in East Point, Georgia, one of my good friends, Lin Price Carter, and I often discussed what we thought our futures might hold. On several occasions, our conversations included talk of the mission field. We both decided that if we never married, we would spend our lives as missionaries—after all, we reasoned, if we couldn't find husbands, we might as well live overseas. We thought this might be a good back-up plan in the event we never became somebody's wives.

Following high school, I headed off to Samford University in Birmingham, Alabama. My first roommate, Leslie Parkman Roe, had been raised on the mission field in the Philippines. Leslie, who had never lived in the States before, taught me so much. Adjusting to American culture was not an easy transition for her. The Lord blessed me, though, by putting the two of us together. Leslie's stories about life in the Philippines and her extensive travels always held my interest and left me with an appetite for experiencing other places. More and more, however, my heart's plans involved marrying, having children, and settling down close to home.

A few years later, I was indeed somebody's wife—I was Mrs. John W. White III. John and I had gotten married, finished college, had our first beautiful baby girl, and now John was halfway through law school. We were living in Birmingham and were active in a wonderful church family. Our life together was moving along according to plan, and we were blissfully content.

One lovely Sunday afternoon we brought Joy Kathryn, our little daughter, home from church, fed her, and put her down for her nap. John and I then prepared to enjoy our lunch together. Once Joy was quiet and we had settled at the table, John said to me, "What would you think if I told you that the Lord was calling me to foreign missions?" Without even blinking an eye, I answered, "I don't think anything of it. God put us together, and if God is going to tell you do to something like that, He's going to have to tell me to do it too. He's surely not going to send one of us without the other. I don't sense God calling me to do that at all." *Besides,* I thought, *that's not part of the plan.* John took my response as an answer from the Lord—maybe he wasn't being called right now after all. He replied, "Okay, well, we'll just wait on that for a while." John, in his wisdom, was not going to force what he perceived to be God's plan on me. He was going to trust God and give Him time to work in the situation.

Over the next two years, I processed what John had said about his sense of call. I watched as God worked in John's life and heart, and after a while, I came to the realization that maybe God had been tugging me toward foreign missions over the years. Yet, my heart was not prepared to embrace the whole idea—not the way John's seemed to be. From then on, whenever missionaries came to our church services to speak about their work, I became upset as I tried to listen. A deep sense of conviction and disquiet rocked my heart. I did not want to be disturbed by this calling—John would soon finish law school, and then we would be free to move back to Atlanta. I had been in Birmingham six years by then, and I was ready to move back near my family, build a home, have more children, kiss John as he headed off to work each morning, and enjoy life as we raised our family around all the people and places that were dear to us. Thinking that those plans might somehow be interrupted troubled me—and, curiously, my anxiety increased sharply whenever visiting missionaries spoke.

To quiet my discomfort, I developed a habit of simply tuning out whenever missionaries shared. If I did pay attention to them, I sensed a tug at my heart that maybe God was pulling me in that direction. But I didn't *want* to be sensitive to His leading in my life, at least not in that area! I thought about other things—anything else to keep my mind from focusing on what the missionaries were saying. That tactic went on for about a year and a half, until finally, we moved home to Atlanta.

My plan had worked! Two years passed in Atlanta. We had a lovely home just ten minutes from my parents and had been blessed with our second child, a boy. John was working at the Chick-fil-A headquarters, and I was living out my dream of being a wife and mother. Yet something wasn't quite right. John and I felt a restlessness that we couldn't quite explain. After all, this is what we had wanted; life was good—why didn't it feel better? From time to time the topic of missions came up. We discussed it, but I was still hesitant. Occasionally the thought crept into my mind that maybe life didn't feel better because we had gone on with our plans at the expense of God's. Then, one day, a day I'll never forget, something happened.

The house was quiet. I had just put the children down for their naps, and I was sitting on the sofa in our den. Music played softly as I enjoyed some time reading my Bible. In truth, it is difficult to write about this time, because God seemed so real and so close that I felt like I could just reach out and touch Him. I sensed strongly that God wanted me to do international work, to serve overseas, and to let Him use me. God made it clear to me in those moments that He had blessed me and gifted me with the ability to raise a family overseas and to work with people from other cultures. The words of the song I had been listening to rang in my heart: "If I could just see the world the way you do, Lord, I know I'd serve you more faithfully." That experience with the

Lord and the words of that song impressed upon me that I needed to look at the world in a different way.

The world wasn't just a place to enjoy and visit; the world needed God's love, and ministry opportunities in other countries were available to John and me. God wanted to open our hearts to these opportunities. That night I told John how God had so powerfully touched my soul that day, and I shared that now I was ready to accept God's plan for our lives. We discussed why accepting the call to foreign missions had been such a hard decision for us. We decided that we had been holding on too tightly to material things, to possessions we'd been given and to our lifestyle. That evening we began making a list of possessions that were precious or valuable to us—things that maybe we were holding on to too tenaciously. We wrote down things like our car, our new home, and even our children and our families. We couldn't bear to think about leaving grandparents, brothers, sisters, our church, and life in Atlanta. We added to our list each night, and together, we'd take it before the Lord and say, "Father, we just want to give all these things back to you because we know they came from you. We don't want to hold on to them so tightly that they keep us from doing what you want us to do." The time came when we needed to take the next step of obedience. We wrote a letter to the Foreign Mission Board in Richmond, Virginia, and told them that although we didn't know anything about being missionaries, we were interested in knowing if God could use us somewhere.

That began our outward process of letting go of our plans and seeking earnestly for God's plans. It would change our lives forever. After having lived overseas as missionaries for ten years, I think both of us would say we would go back and do it again in a heartbeat. God continues to keep our eyes open to needs around the world, and even though our call to missions has taken us down various paths, both internationally and in the States, we still strongly sense that the call will always be a part of our lives as we desire to serve according to our giftedness and within God's plan.

What about you?

Has God ever asked you to do something that you did not exactly want to do? How did you handle that situation? What lessons did you learn as a result of following your will? Or what did you learn by obeying Him even when you didn't feel like it?

PARTNERS FOR LIFE

*This explains why a man leaves his father and mother and
is joined to his wife, and the two are united into one.*
—*Genesis 2:24*

I think it is significant that God speaks of the marriage relationship so early in Genesis. The Word of God begins by placing importance on the covenant relationship between a man and a woman. I suppose that is one reason why my dad discussed the issue of marriage with me so early in my life. When I was just thirteen, Dad and I were walking on New Smyrna Beach, and he asked me if I had thought about the man I would marry one day. I was surprised and told him that I hadn't given it much thought, because I was, after all, just thirteen. He told me I should start thinking about my future husband now because marriage would be one of the most important decisions I would make in my life. Dad challenged me to make a list of attributes I wanted in my future husband. Not long after that conversation, while I was spending some time with the Lord before going to sleep, I began that list. It actually became quite dear to me as I added to and deleted from it. As I matured and dated young men, the list helped me focus on what I felt were the most important characteristics of my future husband. I am thankful for my dad's wisdom and for how that list kept me on the right path...

After my freshman year at Samford University in Birmingham, I came home for the summer. I learned that Chick-fil-A was going to open a new store in Birmingham. The problem was, they had not yet found an operator. Dad approached me with the possibility of accepting that position. The idea of becoming an operator really excited me. Dad agreed to let me take the store under three conditions: (1) after one year, I would turn the store over to another operator and finish my education, (2) I would receive no special treatment just because I was Truett Cathy's daughter, and (3) I would not be allowed to call him crying if something went wrong. I accepted the three conditions and eagerly set about tackling my new challenge at the age of nineteen.

First, I rented an apartment right behind the mall so that I could be close to my store. I understood that I would be spending most of my time there, and I was 100 percent committed to seeing this venture succeed. Next, I needed to begin hiring team members to work in the store with me. I began interviewing people as they responded to our "help wanted" advertisements. One of my interviews was with a fine looking young man. He too was a student at Samford, and my initial impression of him was quite positive. As he filled out the application, I leaned over his shoulder and discovered that his name was John White. I decided right then and there that I wanted to learn more about this John White, but I chose not to hire him on the spot. So my budding interest in him wouldn't appear too obvious, I told him I would call him and let him know about the job.

I called John several days later and offered him the job. Much to my delight, he accepted and came to work for me. The more I saw of John, the more I liked him. He was a hard worker and was polite and helpful to the customers. I had one major problem, however: John was a student at Samford, surrounded by pretty girls every day and having opportunity to date and meet more of them every weekend. I had to do something! I began scheduling John to work every Friday night. I figured that was the best way to keep my eye on him and keep him from other "distractions."

It didn't take long for me to realize that I really enjoyed being around John. We had a great time working together, and the hours seemed to fly. I wanted to spend more time with him, but all of my time was consumed with looking after and running the store. I took another bold step: I slowly began bumping up John's hours more and more each week. He never complained about the extra hours, so I went even further: I scheduled John to work with me every Saturday as well. When he still didn't raise a fuss about the long hours, it dawned on me that he must have enjoyed spending all that time with me just as much as I had enjoyed spending it with him.

Some time later John asked his dad's advice about dating me. John's father told him that it wasn't a good idea—you just don't date your boss. Although a bit reluctant to disregard his dad's advice, John finally worked up the courage to invite me to dinner one Saturday evening. Later I often went to church with him, where he was involved in directing the music. He took me to his home church and introduced me to his parents. We'd go out on official dates but only after closing the store together and making our night deposit. As our relationship became serious, I completed my year's commitment to the store, returned to Samford to continue my studies, and to my delight, became engaged to John the following summer.

John and I celebrated our twenty-fifth anniversary on July 16, 2002. We still enjoy working together and are happiest when we have a task to tackle together—whether it's simply doing the dishes in the evening or teaching a Bible study, we make a great team! Marrying John truly is one of the best decisions I've ever made.

What about you?

If you're married, reflect on the circumstances that brought you and your spouse together. If you are single, reflect on what Jesus said in Matthew 19:11-12. What advantages does a single person have in serving God?

If you desire to be married some day, start a list similar to the one my father challenged me to make. What characteristics do you consider most important in a future spouse?

FAMILY TIES

And as waters fill the sea, so the earth will be filled
with people who know the LORD.

—Isaiah 11:09b

Many families have certain jokes, traditions, and special names or words that only members of their family know. My family is no exception. When we pass a car wreck, we'll more likely say we passed a "bump-em-up" than say we passed an accident. I can identify people who have known my husband for most of his life when I hear them refer to him as Buck—it's a family nickname he earned as a small boy, and only those who have known him since his childhood use this name. What a blessed experience it is, then, to belong to an eternal family. When we accept Jesus Christ as our Lord and Savior, we are ushered into a family that will last forever, sharing one Father. Just like our earthly families, our Christian family shares a special set of experiences, grounded in God's love, that transcend national and linguistic borders.

When we had been in Brazil for just a few days, our colleagues introduced us to a Brazilian woman, Cleuza, who would be helping us in our home. Cleuza had been a Christian for two years, though her husband was not a believer, and they had four children ranging in age from eight to fourteen years old. Cleuza and her family lived in the poorest section of Campinas. The impoverished areas around Brazilian cities, called favelas, are mazes of little shacks, constructed of cardboard, leftover wood, and bits of crumbly brick. Living conditions there are difficult, to say the least, but out of that desperate environment, God brought me a lesson in contentment and love.

In addition to preparing our lunch each day and helping with household chores, Cleuza would have the responsibility of watching our two preschoolers, Joy and John-John, while John and I were away at language school each afternoon. The necessity of leaving the children burdened me; I loved being a mother and wanted to be there for my children, particularly as they adjusted to a foreign place. Initially, I didn't know anything about Cleuza except that she was going to come and care for my children. But now I tell people that it was with Cleuza that I learned my greatest lesson the entire time we were in Brazil: the greatness of God's love and how He makes Himself known to all of His children.

Cleuza and I spent a couple of days together to get better acquainted, allow the children time to become comfortable with her, and so that I could try to com-

municate our routine. We had one problem: she didn't
understand any English, and I didn't understand Portuguese. We spent two days motioning back and forth to
each other as I tried to explain to her how to care for
the children and familiarized her with their schedules.
She accompanied me throughout those two days, ob-
serving what I did with the children and how I did things
around the house. I wanted to let her know that she
should put John-John down for a nap at two o'clock every day. At two that afternoon, I pointed to my watch
and went to get John-John. She nodded to indicate that
she understood she was supposed to get him at two and
put him in his bed. I always spent some time with the
children as they drifted off to sleep each day and at night,
patting them on their backs. I took Cleuza's hand,
stretched it down, and laid it across John-John's back,
and together we patted him. She looked at me and
smiled and nodded, and I smiled back. She understood
what to do when she laid John-John down.

Her friendly, willing manner was such a blessing to
me, but I was still anxious. It was important to me that
the children maintain their regular routine and that
Cleuza do the same sort of things I would do with them.
We were in a strange country with people who looked
and talked differently—something needed to be the
same for the children. I wanted them to have security
and consistency in their daily activities at least. Now
that we had John-John lying down and I felt she under-

stood that I patted him, I attempted to communicate the next little step in our bedtime ritual. I wanted to tell her that I also sang to the children as they fell asleep, but I didn't know if she sang or even knew any songs. I decided to just start singing and see what would happen. I started softly, "Jesus loves me this I know, for the Bible tells me so . . ."At first she just listened to me, but when I got to the chorus, she began singing along with me in Portuguese as I continued in English.

When we finished the song, a revelation struck me. My parents had told me since I was a young girl that God loved people all around the world, and I had long ago memorized John 3:16: "For God so loved *the world* that He gave His only Son, so that everyone who believes in Him will not perish but have eternal life." But for the first time, in those precious moments I shared with Cleuza, it dawned on me how great God truly is and how awesome His love is. For here was a lady standing beside me, speaking a language I could not understand, having lived a life I could not imagine, singing of God's love. At some time in her life, God had reached down into a favela in Campinas and touched her heart, demonstrating His love for her in such a way that she accepted Him and became His child, just as He had touched my heart, thousands of miles away in a small town in Georgia decades earlier. God had never even gone to language school to learn how to communicate with her! Language is no barrier for our heavenly Father. He can call His sons and daughters in any tongue, in any place, at any time.

I understood then that God was—and still is —communicating to people all around the world. At this very moment, He is at work in the hearts and lives of countless people in every corner of the globe. That was a revelation to me, bringing a fresh understanding of the limitless power and love of our Father. There I was, struggling so hard to communicate with people, overwhelmed with the many cultural nuances I would need to master in order to share Christ meaningfully, but God showed me clearly that this was no challenge for Him. As different as Cleuza's and my lives had been, both of us had been made a part of God's family through the blood of Jesus, and we had no problem communicating and understanding an expression of His love.

What about you?

What are some unique traditions, words, or experiences your family shares?

Describe several in detail and tell how these "family ties" create a special closeness in your family relationships.

"ELEPHANTED!"

Happiness or sadness or wealth should not keep anyone from doing God's work. Those in frequent contact with the things of this world should make good use of them without becoming attached to them, for this world and all it contains will pass away.
—*1 Corinthians 7:30-31*

Does change make you uneasy? Perhaps as a child you found it discomfiting to walk into a new classroom each fall, or as a young adult you cringed at the idea of moving to a strange city to begin a new job. As we mature, changes can either become easier, due to our experience and acceptance of them, or they can become ever more difficult as we attempt to keep our life as is. Indeed, changes typically pull us out of our comfort zone sand leave us feeling somewhat like a fish out of water. Just in case you were unaware: when our Lord returns, everything will change in the blink of an eye. This world (with all its comfort zones) will pass away. Why not indulge in some less drastic changes now so your system won't be too shocked then?

When we moved to Brazil in 1984, Southern Baptists, through the Cooperative Program, provided us with a lovely home. John and I often remarked to each other that such a comfortable living space helped see us through many of the difficult adjustments our young family faced. Still, our home required us to get used to some unexpected differences.

Our home in Atlanta had been carpeted. We never appreciated how much carpet muffled the sounds of our two lively preschoolers, Joy and John-John, until we settled into our home in Campinas. With our home's hardwood floors, ceramic tile walls in the kitchen and bathroom, and ten-foot ceilings, we sometimes felt like we were living in an echo chamber! As you can imagine, this situation delighted Joy and John-John as they experimented with a wide variety of new sounds.

Another interesting change we had to adjust to was our hot water heater—or lack thereof! Rather than having a regular drum hot water heater, which luxuriously heats gallons of water at once, we had small heaters attached to our shower heads and kitchen faucet. These little contraptions at least knocked the chill off the water as it poured from the taps. And, though the water came from the tap nice and cold, we had to boil it if we wanted to drink it. I learned that I had taken water—hot, cold, and potable—for granted before coming to Brazil.

City living was also a huge adjustment for us. We moved to Rio de Janeiro in August 1985 after completing our first year of language study in Campinas. Since I had grown up on a farm, surrounded by countryside, with only the mooing of cows and the chatter of birds to interrupt the stillness, I found the noise and excitement of Rio a bit overwhelming. Truthfully, city living tested our patience. Rio is an incredible city with many things to do, but we had to remember that we weren't the only people visiting those attractions. To put it simply, it took us three times longer to do things than we ever thought it would.

Someone once wisely told us, "What bugs you in the States will 'elephant' you overseas." We learned to appreciate that statement. One of my biggest challenges while living in Rio was driving. It required a lot of confidence and an equal amount of aggressiveness. Without these two essential elements, you'd get left behind. John told me, "Trudy, the secret to driving here is just to go with the flow." If the flow went fast, you went fast; if it went slowly, you went slowly. If the flow didn't stop at a red light, you certainly didn't risk it either. There was certainly never a dull moment living in such a big city. If we had not chosen to bend with the changes, we surely would have broken!

While we faced many changes in our living conditions and adjusting to traffic, we endured some social transitions as well. We had to learn the hard way about many Brazilian customs. For example, Brazilians consider it rude to be on time to someone's house for dinner. In fact, the later you arrive, the more polite you are considered. Once when our dinner guests were an hour late, I thought they had gotten lost along the way, but they were simply trying to be polite! Imagine my confusion when they showed up with no explanation or embarrassment over their tardiness. Interestingly, when we returned to the States, we had difficulty breaking this custom. Suddenly we were required to be on time wherever we went (that's not always easy when you're also expected to stop at *every* red light!).

All of these changes, and many more, made us take a closer look at what we had thought was "right" and "proper" and forced us to focus on what was really important. We easily could have become bogged down in longing for wall-to-wall carpet and a hot shower. We could have become increasingly annoyed at the sounds and traffic conditions of the city. I can't pretend that these things didn't bother us, but they did not overshadow why we were there. We weren't in Brazil to be comfortable or happy; we were there to serve the Lord. It was certainly worth all the changes

What about you?

What "elephants" you (really bugs you)? Describe two or three pet peeves, and think about why those things bother you so much. How much control do these "elephants" have over your life? Would these things ever keep you from doing what you know the Lord wants you to do for Him?

NEXT-DOOR NEIGHBORS

*[Jesus said] "You must love the Lord your God with
all your heart, all your soul, and all your mind.
This is the first and greatest commandment.
A second is equally important: Love your
neighbor as yourself. All the other commandments
and all the demands of the prophets are based
on these two commandments."*
—*Matthew 22:37-40*

Do you notice that Jesus tells us in these verses that loving our neighbor is equal in importance to loving God? He doesn't say, "A second is almost as important." Jesus says loving those around us, whether in our neighborhoods, schools, or any other public meeting place, is just as important to God as loving Him. I hope you will enjoy some of our stories about our neighbors . . .

When we first moved to Brazil, my helplessness and confusion at not being able to freely converse with our neighbors almost overwhelmed me. Soon we all began to realize that a friendly smile and wave were good ways to begin communicating. As I gained some confidence, I learned five Portuguese sentences that would allow me to introduce myself. I made some pound cakes and then headed off to use my new sentences, cakes in hand, to reach out to my neighbors. Baked goods and friendly words often go a long way in creating bonds with one's neighbors.

Our street was a playground for all of the neighborhood children. A hopscotch board had been painted on the street, and a cord strung between two trees across the street functioned as a volleyball net. It was a common sight to see a game in progress. Several young girls lived on our street, and Joy enjoyed playing with them. They were fascinated by their new neighbor who spoke a language that was foreign to them.

One afternoon, when Joy was playing, John noticed her run into the house. He was relieved to know that she was okay when she bounded back out to her playmates, moments later, with something in her hands. Curiously, he moved to get a better look at what she had been so eager to get. That's when he saw Joy standing amongst her friends with our Portuguese/English dictionary, flipping through the pages, as if to see what in the world those children were saying to her. Showing a desire to understand others has a way of endearing a person to her neighbors!

Opportunities to share God's love with others, especially in the area of physical hunger and material needs, were numerous in Brazil. In fact, hardly a week went by without children and adults coming to our gate asking for bread to eat or cardboard boxes to use as floors in their homes. One day, as I drove up to the house, six little children were in the front yard. They were in the process of opening our trash bag, hoping to find something to eat. Immediately, I was reminded of the Scripture, "Lord, when did we see you hungry, and feed You, or thirsty, and give You drink?" (Matt. 25:37). I fed the hungry children a meal of rice, beans, fruit, and bread. Facing and responding to the most basic needs of those around us is one of the essential elements of neighborliness.

§ § §

Lest you think we've only been on the giving end, I want to share with you some times when our neighbors reached out to us. Just next door to us lived a Hindu family who spoke English quite well. In our early days in Brazil, they were a wonderful help to us—truly a blessing. John became friends with the man in that family, and they often went for walks together in the evening around our neighborhood so they could talk and familiarize John with the surroundings. One night as they strolled along, they were startled by an angry dog charging at them. Just as the dog was about to jump on John and bite him from behind, our Hindu neighbor whipped off his belt and slapped that dog silly. Rather than looking out for his own welfare—after all, he could have taken off running—our neighbor bravely put himself in harm's way and protected John against what probably would have been a painful injury. He demonstrated neighborliness by watching someone else's back (literally!).

§ § §

After we moved to Richmond, I experienced some bouts of loneliness. I didn't know anyone in Richmond and felt isolated. John's new job responsibilities included a good deal of travel, so I frequently found myself at home alone with the children. Not long after we moved into our new home, our eldest son, John-John, broke his leg. John carried him up our steep stairs each evening so that John-John could go to bed. Well, it just so happened that John had to go out of town, and I remembered wondering how on earth I was going to get my thirteen-year-old son up those steps—he was bigger than me! That evening, Maurice and Laurie Graham and their two sons, Peter and Aaron, came by for a visit. Maurice was the associate pastor at our new church home, Bon Air Baptist, and they had stopped by to welcome us and chat. Their visit encouraged me, since John was away. As they were preparing to leave, Maurice told me to call him if I needed anything and asked if he could do anything for me before they left. I looked over at John-John on the couch and explained that I didn't quite know how I was going to get him up to bed. Without another word, Maurice and his sons whisked John-John off the couch and up the stairs. Being a good neighbor sometimes involves a strong back and a willing spirit!

What about you?

Write about a time in your life when you had the opportunity to be kind or helpful to one of your neighbors. What did you do? How did your neighbor respond to your kind or helpful deed? Also describe a time when your neighbors came to your assistance.

ADVANCE TEAM

*Do not be afraid or discouraged, for the LORD is the
one who goes before you. He will be with you; he
will neither fail you nor forsake you.*
—Deuteronomy 31:8

Whenever the president of the United States travels, his advance team always arrives days before him. Their job involves planning the president's travel routes, preparing office space for his staff, investigating the backgrounds of those who will be serving him, searching and securing his accommodations, and preparing the hosts for their venerable visitor. As Christians, we can rest assured that our heavenly Father is meticulous about preparing our way ahead as well. He can remove any danger, give us grace to handle any situation, and prepare a place for us where, we too, can lay our heads in safety . . .

One Saturday night in the spring of 1984, my husband, John, and I, along with our two small children, Joy and John-John, climbed aboard a plane bound for Miami to begin our lives as missionaries in Brazil. With our eyes red and puffy from the tears of a heartbreaking farewell, we tried our best to settle our two little ones and to focus on the journey ahead. The Lord had prepared us for this moment, and He was faithful to give us the courage to say our final goodbye and the grace to trust in His plan.

Arriving in Miami, we shepherded our little family to the next plane we would board, destined for Bolivia. Hours later, we would perform the same task again, except on foreign soil, to catch our flight to Paraguay. But the trip was not over yet; we still had to fly into Brazil. As you can imagine, we were very happy to finally arrive. Though we had not spent forty years wandering through a desert, that trip gave us greater compassion for the wayward Israelites! God was in the details then, and He was in the details of our journey as well. We made all of our connections and, without our knowledge or input, He prepared our way upon our arrival.

We will always remember Easter Sunday 1984 as a special day. We landed in São Paulo, Brazil, at four o'clock in the afternoon. John and I had asked friends and family to pray for us to have an easy time of clearing customs. In 1984, video cameras were somewhat of a novelty, and we were concerned that ours might be confiscated. By divine appointment, a little man in an official uniform helped us as we got off the plane. He stayed with us until we cleared customs, correcting some of our forms, and even finding a place for the children and me to sit while John waited on the luggage. There was never a good explanation for why this man chose to help us in such an extraordinary way, but John and I both agreed that the Lord had done the advance work necessary. We recalled God's promise: "For He will give His angels charge concerning you, to guard you in all your ways" (Psalm 91:11-12). Needless to say, we cleared customs, belongings intact, without any trouble.

Exiting the customs lounge, we were greeted by colleagues and three missionary families who had been in Brazil since January. We made a lively caravan traveling the sixty miles to Campinas, Sao Paulo. Our excitement mounted as we drew closer to "home." Months of eager anticipation would soon give way to living experience as we saw our new community for the first time. Our colleagues helped us carry our luggage into the house, gave us keys to our car, and even provided us with the essentials for our first night in this foreign land. That night as we laid our heads on our pillows, we experienced a peace and security that comes only from the Lord. We knew, beyond a doubt, that we had been completely obedient to God's direction and that He had come before us to prepare the way.

What about you?

Describe a time in your life when you have clearly seen God's provision for you unfolding. Perhaps you feel you have never experienced this. Think for a moment about a time when friends, family, or complete strangers have come to your aid at just the right moment, called or made an effort to cheer you up at just the right time, or have provided for some need in just the right way. Could it be possible that God used them as part of His advance team?

A MATTER OF WAITING

*Be still in the presence of the L*ORD *and*
wait patiently for him to act.

—*Psalm 37:7*

Isn't waiting hard enough without being reminded
that we are to wait patiently? Waiting, if you think
about it, doesn't require much—you don't have to do
or say anything; you just wait. Can you even imagine
how many square feet of space across America are dedicated to waiting rooms—in hospitals, car repair shops,
airports, hair salons? The truth is, we should be pretty
good at waiting, and we all know how to wait, but I
doubt we all wait "well." Developing patience takes
waiting to a whole new level. Waiting patiently in
matters of the heart requires trust and practice. As
we trust God's wisdom to guide us, He will give us opportunities to develop and exercise patient waiting.

Shortly after arriving in Brazil, John and I decided we
were ready to have another child. Although we were experiencing many changes, adjusting to Brazil and attend-

ing language school every day, we felt a strong desire to enlarge our family. In July 1984, I was thrilled by the possibility that I might be pregnant. I was greatly disappointed to realize that it was a false alarm. Several months of waiting passed and my anxiety grew. By December I was feeling rather low.

Then I read Colossians. As I read those words, I realized that I had not been permitting God's peace about this situation to enter into my life. John often told me I needed to come to the point where I could admit and know for certain that God knows what is best for our family. I began to realize that our desire for a child at that time was not necessarily God's design for our family. God used this experience to teach me a lot about time—not my time, but His. Accepting the answer "no" from God about something I so badly wanted was hard.

During that time, I was reminded of something special about the two precious children we already had, Joy and John-John. We had a little girl and a little boy not because John and I planned it but because God had chosen to give them to us. Our children are gifts from God. They are part of His plan. It dawned on me that if and when I did get pregnant it would be God's will, God's timing, and God's design. I could (and should) relax, knowing this situation was in very capable hands.

After ten months of waiting (admittedly not always patient waiting), we were ecstatic to learn that I was pregnant. We were overjoyed with the news, but even more than that, I was grateful to God for the opportunity to have learned more about how He works in my life. He never forces Himself into our lives, but rather, we must choose to receive the peace that only He can give. When we do, anxious waiting can turn into sweet and patient abiding.

I learned that God's timing is always better than ours. Had I been pregnant when I wanted to be, I would have had difficulty spending the time needed to learn the language and culture of Brazil. Making all the adjustments of coming to the mission field, a major life change, would have been hard on my body. The Lord may answer our prayers in three different ways: yes, no, or wait. Whatever the response, it is the best response for that time.

This story wouldn't be complete if I didn't share that our waiting was well worth it. Our precious baby girl, Angela Jeannette, was born September 14, 1985 in Rio de Janeiro, Brazil. Indeed, God makes all things beautiful (and all beautiful things) in *His* time.

§ § §

Angela was home schooled until the fourth grade, when our family returned to the States. In May 2003, she graduated from Trinity Episcopal High School in Richmond, Virginia. I am proud to share that she received the Bishop's Award for Character and Integrity from the faculty of Trinity. Angela is currently a student at Union University in Jackson, Tennessee.

What about you?

Have you ever wanted something so much that the desire almost consumed you? How did you deal with that? Describe a time in your life when you had to wait for a goal to be accomplished, a dream to be fulfilled, or a deep want to be satisfied. What did you learn as a result of that time of waiting?

SHIPWRECKS, SHARKS, AND SHORTS

So take courage! For I believe God.
It will be just as he said.
But we will be shipwrecked on an island.
—*Acts 27:25-26*

Do the preceding verses make you chuckle a bit? Paul entreats his companions to take heart and have faith in God. He follows up this encouragement with an aside: By the way, we're going to be marooned on an island. The flow of thoughts here might be considered strangely ironic to some, but I believe it is good instruction on how to live a life of faith in the midst of obstacles. Paul was focused on the surety of God's promises, not on the difficulties lying in wait along the way to their fulfillment. . .

Our first year in Brazil was filled with joy and frustration. The joy and excitement of knowing we were in

God's will and learning to live and serve in a new culture were often exhilarating. But with our highs came some lows. Learning a new language and adapting to new surroundings and customs while raising a family is not easy. One of our primary objectives during that first year in Brazil was to become proficient in communicating in Portuguese. We had faith that God would make this possible, but we certainly experienced our share of "shipwrecks" along the way.

I must admit, some of these linguistic wrecks were disheartening. But God gave us the grace to laugh at ourselves. These humbling experiences brought us closer to the Lord and to the Brazilians who witnessed them. In our struggle to learn their language, they did not see us as self-sufficient Americans who were there for the purpose of helping and teaching them; instead they recognized that we were vulnerable and needed their help. I hope you will enjoy a good laugh with us as you read about the following "shipwrecks."

It was the first week of December in 1984, and we were about to host six Americans who were coming to work in our church. The Sunday before they were to arrive, one of our members approached me and said she was in charge of coordinating the meals. She had written down my name for two evenings, and when she showed me the menu plan for my first meal, it read: *"Carne—cachorro quinte."* I interpreted this to mean "dog meat—hot." Trying to keep my composure, I said, as politely as my Portuguese would allow, "I'm sorry, but I've never had this before, and I'm not sure how to prepare it."

She responded, "Don't Americans eat this?"

I answered, "No, I really don't think they do. I'd be glad to fix something else, though."

She seemed somewhat surprised but went along with my suggestion. Later that week, after sharing the conversation with my language school professor, I discovered that the words on the menu had simply meant "hot dogs"!

§ § §

My eldest daughter, Joy, was four years old when we arrived in Brazil. She was quite adept with English and soon learned many Portuguese words at her Brazilian preschool. Her learning curve quickly surpassed her parents', and it wasn't long before I was taking her along on shopping trips as a language helper. Joy has always enjoyed leading, so this was a natural role for her. In fact, one time, when I decided to leave her at home and venture out on my own, she called after me, "Mommy, are you sure you'll be okay? You won't need my help, will you?" That comment from the mouth of a four-year-old could easily have shipwrecked my confidence, but it did make me appreciate how humbling a situation I was in.

On one occasion, when Joy was five, she did accompany me. We were busily going about our shopping when I realized there was an item on my list that I did not know how to ask for. Undaunted, I told Joy what I needed in English, and she gave me the Portuguese word. I looked at the clerk and repeated what Joy had said. The woman looked at me with a confused expression, saying she did not understand. I turned to Joy and asked her to tell me again what the word was. She repeated the same thing. I assumed my accent must have been off on my first attempt, so I tried again. Still, the woman was clueless. With that, I looked down at Joy, and she had her mouth covered, giggling. She had made up a word and enjoyed a good joke at my expense!

Being the object of a five-year-old's joke was a bit unsettling; some might even let that even wreck their day. I looked down at that little face, so full of amusement, and I thought, *Great, now even my own child has turned against me!* But I did find some satisfaction in knowing that my preschooler exhibited enough intelligence to so completely fool her mother.

§ § §

One of John's favorite new experiences in Brazil was shopping in the street markets. He headed out on Saturday mornings and often brought home traditional Brazilian foods for us all to try. One particular morning, he ran into a little trouble with one of his purchases. He wanted to buy some shark meat, which we had heard was delicious. After searching the stalls of the market, he came upon a fish stand that had reasonable prices able prices and fresh merchandise. When he got the clerk's attention, he attempted to place his order. But, instead of using the word for *shark,* he used another word that is quite similar in Portuguese. He told the clerk he wanted to buy "one kilo of shorts, please." The clerk's reaction was enough to let John know that he had made a mistake. Recovering from fits of laughter, the clerk corrected John's word choice and sent him on his way with a kilo of shark meat.

What about you?

What's the funniest thing you have ever said or done? Take a few moments and write about what happened in detail. If you remember a particularly funny incident that involved a loved one, write it down too. Often these stories become cherished family memories, and they provide enjoyment for everyone. Write them down!

A GREAT CELEBRATION: GOD WITH US

Because of God's tender mercy, the light from heaven
is about to break upon us, to give light to those
who sit in darkness and in the shadow of death,
and to guide us to the path of peace.

—Luke 1:78-79

Does any other day evoke such strong feelings and remembrances as Christmas? Whether our emotions and memories are intensely joyful or desperately sad, Christmas touches us deeply. I wonder what Joseph and Mary would say about that first Christmas. Surrounded by the odor of animals, without a clean or comfortable place for Mary to labor, away from home and family, their situation was far from ideal. Yet shepherds came with great joy to celebrate Baby Jesus' birth. A star shone brightly to herald the birth of the King. And scripture tells us that Mary "quietly treasured these things in her heart and thought about them often" (Luke 2:19). Should we too learn to look past our surroundings and circumstances on each Christmas Day and treasure in our hearts "the Light from heaven" that came down to light our way to salvation?

Our first Christmas in Brazil proved a difficult time of testing for me. Christmas is one of my favorite times of year, but spending Christmas in a foreign country, thousands of miles from extended family members, felt quite lonely at times. Songs like "I'll Be Home for Christmas" and "There's No Place Like Home for the Holidays" left me with a big lump in my throat and a longing to be back in America. Compounding this sense of distance was the fact that Christmas in Brazil came in the dead of summer. The intense heat did little to remind us of the cold weather we associated with Christmas. I began thinking about the essence of our celebration of Christmas and the source of its joy.

One night I read an article titled "The One Farthest from Home." It mentioned the many people who were far away from home on that first Christmas long ago. Though Mary and Joseph returned to the home of their ancestors, Bethlehem must not have felt quite like home since they had to stay in a stable. The wise men, too, left their homes to follow a star. But, without a doubt, the One farthest from home was Jesus. He left His home in heaven so that He might make heaven our home.

As I reflected further, the realization occurred to me that our family was far away from home that year so that we could let people know about the home Jesus had made for them. We had the opportunity to give the most precious Christmas gift of all to the people to whom God had called us to minister. It dawned on me that perhaps being away from home was part of the true meaning of Christmas. If Jesus hadn't left His home in heaven, there would be no Christmas to celebrate! Furthermore, if Christ's people did not reach out beyond their homes, beyond safe and comfortable zones, many would never hear of the home He has for them.

As the years went by, our Christmases in Brazil became less and less foreign to us. We acquired an artificial tree from another missionary family, and each December, we took our tree out on our porch to decorate it. Dressed in shorts and flip-flops, we sang along with Christmas music from America playing in the background as we decorated the tree in the relative comfort of our breezy porch. We talked to the children about the winter cold and snow our family in the States was experiencing. The youngest child then put cotton balls on the tree to make it look like snow had fallen. After decorating the tree, we would slide it back inside the house and sit down for a cool drink. Our little Angela was fascinated with the lights and ornaments and often fell asleep on her back, head under the boughs of the tree, gazing up at the lights from below. Although those Christmases never replaced our memories of Christmas back home in the States, we grew to appreciate them for their uniqueness.

Christmas in Brazil, like the world over, is commercialized. Stores were filled with green and red decorations, colored lights, and toys. In Brazilian homes, families carefully decorated little artificial trees with special ornaments.

Like Americans, Brazilians love to be with their families. Often several families gather at Christmastime to celebrate. Once we made our final move to Brasilia, families from our church took turns adopting us each Christmas, insisting that we join in their celebrations. They began the celebration at midnight on Christmas Eve with a large dinner followed by a gift exchange. The tradition was for each person to bring one gift for the individual whose name they had drawn earlier in the week. One by one, everyone stood and gave clues about the person whose name he or she had drawn, recalling special events, qualities, or characteristics of that person. Giving the hints was almost more fun than actually giving the gift. Whoever opened a gift was the next to give clues, and this process continued until everyone had received a present. The festivities usually lasted until around four in the morning, and families typically rested on Christmas Day.

For our Brazilian brothers and sisters in Christ, Christmas was not so much a time of gift giving as it was a celebration of Jesus' birth. Families enjoyed attending worship services, reading the Christmas story, singing hymns, and praying together. All of the Baptist churches had a program on Christmas night with varying degrees of grandeur. No matter on what day of the week Christmas fell—even if it was a Monday and everyone had already been in church the previous day—the churches were packed for the service on the twenty-fifth.

Where you are, who you are with, what you are doing–these factors do not dictate the spirit and joy of Christmas. The spirit and joy of Christmas was established for all time in a humble stable in Bethlehem, long before the first Christmas song or tradition was ever shared.

What about you?

Consider the following statement for a moment, then complete it. Don't answer the way you think *you should, but be honest with yourself.*

"It just wouldn't be Christmas if we ..."

What are some practical ways you can remind your family and friends of the true meaning of Christmas?

WET FEET

Indeed, God is ready to help you right now.
Today is the day of salvation.

—*2 Corinthians 6:2*

How many times have you heard the expressions "You don't get something for nothing" or "There's no such thing as a free lunch"? Wouldn't you say the thoughts that give rise to such words are fairly common to the American psyche? As a people, Americans find it difficult to accept the concept of being given something freely, with no strings attached. In fact, the idea of being given something we didn't earn can make some of us downright uncomfortable! It goes against the American work ethic and the fierce independence upon which we pride ourselves. We live in a do-it-yourself society that makes us feel weak if we ask for help. But did you know that your eternal life depends upon your decision to accept help—the help of Jesus Christ to bridge the chasm between you and your heavenly Father? And you know what? It's free! Will you accept it?

While on a fishing trip in Central Brazil, my husband, John; our son John-John; and a few friends were enjoying the beauty of the Brazilian countryside. It was a good opportunity to get away from the hustle and bustle of the city and appreciate the peace a few days of fishing can bring. And the trip started out that way too—just a few men and a little boy, telling jokes and impressing one another with stories of big catches gone by. After loading their little boat with tackle boxes, coolers, and rods, they were off.

Being the serious fishermen that they were, the men soon became engrossed in choosing just the right spot to anchor their boat. As they scanned the waters to find that sweet spot where the fish waited unsuspectingly for a meal, suddenly their attention turned swiftly to a loud scraping noise beneath them. Within moments they realized that their boat had been snagged and punctured by a hidden stump lying just beneath the surface of the water. Suddenly a peaceful fishing trip turned into a raucous commotion as water quickly filled the boat. John-John screamed, lifting his feet, "Dad, I don't want to get my feet wet!"

Fortunately, John-John was wearing a life vest, and John threw him out of the boat into the open water. The rest of the fishing party soon followed, and the boat flipped over, dumping their gear into the water. Everything in the boat sank—battery, fishing rods, and tackle boxes. The men worked to stay afloat and swim to shore, with John-John floating effortlessly beside them.

A few young Brazilian boys who happened to be nearby witnessed the entire incident. They volunteered to dive for the lost gear. The men gratefully accepted their offer. The boys were able to recover everything but the tackle boxes. The end result of a four-day fishing adventure: a boat with a hole, a few fish, and a great illustration of how God works in our lives.

John-John was wearing a life vest, so he was prepared for the crisis. His dad had given him the vest and told him to wear it as a safety precaution. John-John didn't have to pay his dad for the vest; he just gave it to him. When John threw him into the water, John-John believed that the vest would hold him up. He didn't fight against it or insist on swimming into shore himself—he wouldn't have been able to anyway, as the distance was too great for his little body. The other men in the boat also had confidence in life vests, but they had chosen not to put one on. They believed that they would return from their fishing expedition in the same boat they left in. They certainly didn't expect to have to swim back to shore on their own power.

§ § §

John-John began his senior year at Auburn University in the fall of 2003. He has been vigorous in his desire and efforts to share the love of Christ with his peers at Auburn. He became a member of the Auburn football team as a walk-on and is dedicated to the rigors of working out as a punter for the Tigers. It has been a great pleasure for his father and me to watch him fulfill one of his dreams. John has demonstrated such character as he has remained committed to the team even when obstacles and circumstances have made it difficult. His guiding passion is to encourage young athletes to know God —even if it means getting his feet wet!

§ § §

Many people today claim they believe in God. Some may even go to church and read their Bibles. But unlike John-John, who accepted his dad's offer of a life vest, they haven't yet accepted the free offer that will save their souls.

If you haven't accepted Jesus as your personal Savior and trusted your life into God's hands, you can do so right now. You see, this illustration breaks down at one extremely crucial point: though the men in this story could swim ashore and save themselves, the only way you can receive eternal salvation is by accepting the gift Jesus freely offers. God is ready to help you right now.

What about you?

At what point in your life did trusting God become important to you? When did you abandon striving on your own and/or depending on other people and just trust God with your needs, hurts, and joys? If you haven't reached this point yet, what is stopping you? Reread the verse that opens this devotion. Write about your thoughts.

IT'S ALL ABOUT THE BODY

*All the believers met together constantly and
shared everything they had. They sold their possessions
and shared the proceeds with those in need. They
worshiped together at the Temple each day, met in
homes for the Lord's Supper, and shared their meals
with great joy and generosity—all the while praising
God and enjoying the goodwill of all the people.*
—Acts 2:44-47a

We can't go many places where everyone is considered to be on equal footing. The second our babies are born, they are weighed and their potential for health is judged. Once we are in school, we are graded and assessed to determine whether we are bright, average, or slow. On the playing fields, the discovery is quickly made about who is fast and agile, and who is slow or clumsy. As adults, our job defines our importance to and place in society. Doctors are usually afforded more respect than ditch diggers. Is there any place we can go where we are not rated, evaluated, and classified? Within our church families, we should be able to find just such a place. God is no respecter of person or station in life. He values the heart of the ditch digger the same as that of the doctor. Our worship in Brazil taught us a great deal about how level God's field is . . .

Right from the beginning nothing thrilled John and me more than praising the Lord with our Brazilian brothers and sisters in Christ, even in Portuguese. When we first arrived in Brazil, we attended a church of about fifty members, with an average attendance of eighty people. This church ministered to the poorer areas of Campinas. One thing was certain: we never had to worry about parking problems. Most of the members walked to church.

Watching mothers carry their young children miles to church deepened our own faith. These women loved Jesus so much, they willingly suffered inconveniences to have the opportunity to worship Him. When we gave those little children juice and crackers during Sunday school, we knew it might be all they would have to eat that entire day. Coming to terms with that fact was not easy. And yet, when those believers sang, "It is well with my soul," we were humbled beyond words and felt privileged to be among them. God shed joy in their hearts just as richly, maybe more so, than in the finest assemblies.

Our Brazilian pastor and his wife, along with a retired schoolteacher, had started the church three years before we arrived. The congregation had been meeting in a warehouse and was in the process of building a chapel on a small lot next door. They planned to use the warehouse for educational space. We came at an exciting time in the life of this church and were eager to help and watch that little church grow.

Immediately after our first Sunday morning service, the pastor asked me if I could play the organ. All I could do at that point was nod and smile, and I was given the job on the spot. I played for the adults and the children when they sang from then on. That night, the pastor called on John to lead the music. And, you guessed it, John became the music director for both the morning and evening services. Unlike churches in the States, at this church the night service was the main service. The people dressed up, and typically attendance was greater on Sunday night. God's Spirit could be felt in that warehouse church every much as it could be in a grand cathedral.

In March 1985, John reached an important milestone: he preached his first sermon in Portuguese, speaking on the work of the Holy Spirit in the life of the believer. With all prejudice aside, he did an outstanding job. That's my husband! Seriously, his message came across clearly and powerfully. John had worked hard to prepare for his message. Speaking for thirty minutes in a new language, particularly on matters of such importance, was no easy task. But God was faithful and blessed that service.

Shortly after completing language school, we moved to Rio de Janeiro. Following the birth of our second daughter, Angela, in 1985, we strongly felt the Lord directing us to join a small church near our home. The church was comprised of sixty members meeting in a three-story house. Our first Sunday in Bible study was quite an experience. The entire congregation gathered in the tiny sanctuary, dispersed around the room on about twenty pews. It was a bit surprising to see three classes going on simultaneously in such a small space. The noise and activity were somewhat distracting, but we soon adjusted and were able to turn off the other classes and listen to our own teacher. While this arrangement was somewhat distracting, it also had advantages—if you didn't like your teacher, you could just tune in to a teacher from another class. God's wisdom and truths can be communicated regardless of the surroundings or apparent distractions.

In 1987, we were attending yet another new church. Most of us expect showers of blessings in church, but we received showers of *concrete* one Wednesday night! During prayer meeting the heavens opened up, and concrete began to fall in the middle of the room. The support had given way while the men were pouring the second-floor beam. Needless to say, the prayer meeting was disrupted, but it will certainly never be forgotten. I'm happy to say that everyone went away unscathed from this earth-shaking prayer meeting. Our confidence in God hearing our prayers was not shaken, however. We were sure of His presence, even in that little church that would never have passed a codes department inspection elsewhere in the world.

Whether we were worshiping or praying with our Brazilian brothers and sisters, directing music or writing musicals, teaching or learning, preaching or baptizing new believers, we loved being part of the body of Christ in Brazil. To this day we enjoy singing hymns from our Brazilian hymnal as a family, and the children still listen to praise music we bring back on CDs from Brazil. Indeed, we truly enjoyed the goodwill of the Brazilian people and feel privileged to have become part of them and to have had them become an important part of who we are now.

What about you?

Describe a rich spiritual experience you have had with other believers. What made that experience memorable and meaningful? If you do not belong to a body of believers, what thoughts do the verses at the beginning of this devotion evoke? What talents, gifts, and interests might you share with others?

HELPLESS BUT NOT HOPELESS

God has made everything beautiful for its own time.
He has planted eternity in the human heart, but
even so, people cannot see the whole scope of God's
work from beginning to end.

—Ecclesiastes 3:11

If you are old enough to be reading this, I know you have lived long enough to have experienced a painful event. It might be something significant, like the death or illness of a loved one, being the victim of violence, or another of life's tragedies. Or, it could be something that other people may see as less significant, like being turned down at the university you wanted to attend or having your car stolen.

Whatever the event, we all have experienced sad or scary times in our lives. God has a way of refining our experiences and turning them into useful tools that mold us and draw us closer to Him. Usually we don't understand their importance in shaping us until well past the event; perhaps we'll never fully understand them this side of eternity. But the Lord does . . .

On March 18, 1987, John and I headed for the hospital in Rio de Janeiro, full of expectation. I was well past my due date for the birth of our fourth child. Going past my due date was nothing unusual for me, since I had carried Joy, John-John, and Angela longer than full term.

At that time in Brazil, when a woman reached her due date and had not had her baby, doctors induced labor. Most Brazilian women had Cesareans to avoid the pain of natural childbirth. My desire to have our baby naturally was quite uncommon. I had explained to the obstetrician who would deliver our fourth child that childbirth was a team effort for John and me. Since he had delivered Angela, he was accustomed to my unique wishes and even let John be present during labor and delivery.

My labor was induced with our fourth child, and like my labor with our other children, was long and difficult. Finally David Edward was born, but unlike our other babies, all was not well with him. During childbirth the oxygen supply to his brain had been completely cut off; David had asphyxiated.

The moment David was born, I knew immediately that something was wrong with him because he didn't look like my other newborn children. He was a deep purple, almost black, and his little body looked lifeless. When my other children were born, the nurses had let me hold them for a few minutes, but they didn't give David to me at all. Instead they whisked him over to a corner of the room and began working on him. We didn't hear him cry or see him move. Our pediatrician, Dr. Gracie, a British native who had been present during David's birth, worked in the corner with the other physicians, trying to coax some sign of life from his little body. For the first thirty minutes of his life, David did not breathe on his own.

I was left alone on the delivery table with John standing beside me. He put his hands on each side of my head. We both knew, without having to say a word, that something was terribly wrong with our little David. John began to repeat, "The Lord is my Shepherd; the Lord is my Shepherd, I shall not want." Those were the only words he could speak, and he repeated them over and over directly into my face, trying to help me focus on the Lord rather than on what was happening with David. Meanwhile, the medical team worked on David for about thirty minutes.

I don't know whether they gave me a sedative or not, but I drifted in and out of consciousness. The next thing I remember is waking up in a room with John by my side. He began talking to me, explaining that David's life was in jeopardy and that he needed to be moved to another hospital with the facilities and staff to care for critically ill newborns. The medical team had asked whether I wanted to be moved to the same hospital. I said yes, I wanted to be near my baby.

So they put David in one ambulance with several doctors, and me and John in another one, for the trip to the other hospital. That was my first ambulance ride, and it was quite an experience. The roads in that part of Rio were not at all smooth. Having just given birth, my body was sensitive to every little jolt and jerk. It wasn't a joy ride, to say the least. The clinic where we were heading was far up on a hillside, and the only road leading there was paved in cobblestones!

As it turned out, that clinic was like a little haven God had planned for us. David received outstanding care, and the attention was phenomenal. The clinic was just a secluded, humble looking place. We didn't know anything about its reputation, and based on the looks of the place, you wouldn't imagine that its staff could have done much for David. But it was a great place.

David and I settled in. To that point I hadn't seen David except for when he was born, and I certainly hadn't yet touched or held him. He was holding his own, though he had had a rough night and the doctors and nurses were concerned about the possibility of him having another convulsion, since he had experienced one already. The staff gave us hourly reports on his status.

On about the third day, the doctor came by to sign my hospital release form. I was ready to go home, but I wasn't feeling well. I attributed my discomfort to the emotional strain of what we were going through —not knowing whether David would survive. The thought had crossed my mind that something wasn't quite right with me, but I had dismissed that thought amid everything that was happening.

As my mother was helping me walk down the hall to leave the hospital, I suddenly collapsed, and they took me back to my room. The doctors scurried to attend to me. Soon they told us I needed emergency surgery because I was bleeding internally. My situation didn't look good at all. By then my dad and John were there, along with Dr. Gracie. John was trying to interpret for my parents what the doctors were saying at the same time he was trying to listen to them. Dr. Gracie pulled my parents aside to explain the situation to them in English so that John could focus better on the doctors and me. Unexpectedly, now I was in critical condition and they didn't know what the outcome would be. They didn't know how long I had been bleeding and were uncertain about what they would find in surgery. Dr. Gracie offered to go into the operating room with me—she would speak English to try to alleviate some of my stress. She was a great comfort to me.

Dr. Gracie was able to go in and out of the operating room to communicate with John and my parents about how I was doing and what they were finding. Here we had David holding onto life by a thread, and now my life was at stake too. The last thing I heard in surgery was Dr. Gracie saying to me, "This may mean a hysterectomy for you. But I want you to know that you have four wonderful children, and God has blessed you. If you don't have any more, you should be happy with the four you have." Then I went to sleep, not knowing what was going to happen.

I ended up having a hysterectomy, and everything went well. They finished and wheeled me back into my room. I began the long journey of recovery from having a child and a hysterectomy within days of each other. In the meantime, we were very concerned about David.

David had good days and bad ones. Finally, when he was thirteen days old, I regained enough strength to be able to go in and see him for the first time since his birth. The nurses had me scrub down, and they wheeled me into his room. David was in an incubator, and I was just able to reach my finger through and rub his little arm a bit. Of course, I wasn't allowed to hold him. He was in no condition to be lifted, and he was hooked up to all kinds of monitors—they even had wires attached to his head. David's head had been shaved wherever something was hooked up, so he looked rather pitiful. I was relieved to see him breathing, though, and to see at least a little color in that tiny face and body. It was just so special for me to be able to see and touch him. They let me go in once or twice a day after that. Days passed and my body began healing. They let John take me home, but David stayed in the hospital until he was twenty-four days old. We went to visit him every day and eventually I was even able to nurse him. The time came when we were able to take him out of the incubator and hold him.

Those were very difficult times, but we were bathed in prayer by our colleagues, Brazilian friends, and our loved ones back in the States.

One man in particular, Andre, who was from Mozambique and lived in Brazil, had been praying for David every day. As he did so, he would write down a promise from the Bible for David and put that promise in a little box. When we brought David home from the hospital, Andre came by to see this "miracle child" that God had healed and restored. Andre was quite a prayer warrior, so when he took little David in his hands and lifted him up to the Lord, thanking God that He had restored David's life, we were all greatly touched.

David blossomed at home. He strengthened and grew at such a rate that even the doctors were astounded. When he was six months old, we returned to the States with David to have him tested. The doctors stated that developmentally, David was just like any other child his age. In later testing, doctors claimed that, given the trauma of his birth, David should not have been able to do what he was doing. He should have been affected in some way; they could offer no explanation for his remarkable recovery. But we could. We shared the mighty power of God with them—David was well and thriving because God had chosen to heal him. I really believe that even if God had chosen to take David home as a newborn, we still would have come away with a deeper dependence on God and a greater realization that He is in control of every circumstance, even when we cannot grasp its purpose at the time.

§ § §

As of this writing, David is a happy, healthy teenager. He has endless energy and throws himself into life with gusto. David is an accomplished and talented musician, playing the piano, violin, saxophone, and guitar. He loves sports and plays on his school soccer and football teams, enjoying basketball and golf in his free time. David is passionate about the Lord, reminding us often by his words and actions that we need to be about the Lord's work—not just concerned with the here and now. He truly has eternity planted in his heart.

What about you?

Describe an experience in your life that left you feeling totally helpless. What emotions did you encounter as the situation seemed to spin out of control? If you knew the Lord at the time, how did He comfort you? If you do not know the Lord, write about how you get through life's crises on your own. Have you ever thought there just might be "something more" to this life?

THE POOR

As for me, I am poor and needy, but the Lord
is thinking about me right now.

—Psalm 40:17a

These words from the Psalms call us back to the reality of our Father's intimate concern for us. What could be more breathtaking than to understand that the Creator holds each of us in His thoughts? It is helpful to remember this truth whenever we come into contact with people who have experienced hardships—whether as the result of their choices, unfortunate circumstances, or emotional or physical pain. Whatever the cause of their great need, they remain near to God's heart . . .

In May 1990, John and I were actively engaged in ministry in Brazil. We had grown to love the Brazilian people and rejoiced as more and more responded to God's love. One group I felt particularly led to minister to was young mothers. When I say young, I mean quite young. In Brazil it is common to see girls at a very young age caring for their own children. I felt a strong desire to encourage these young mothers, share some of my experience in child rearing with them, and most importantly, to open their eyes to the love of God.

One of the girls that John and I knew was Maria. Maria was nineteen years old and lived with a young man, Manoel, who worked for a construction firm. Maria and Manoel lived at the construction sites until the work was completed. There was no construction trailer or other sound structure for them to live in—their living conditions were rustic at best. Maria had grown up on a farm and had never had the opportunity to go to school. Consequently, she could neither read nor write. She had lost her first baby when she was eighteen and had recently given birth to her second child, Ana.

When Maria went into labor with Ana, Manoel had come to our home and awakened us in the middle of the night. Groggy from having been called unexpectedly from bed, John woke up enough to drive them to the hospital. He returned shortly thereafter. The next morning, Manoel told us that Maria had been turned away at the hospital John had taken them to and that they caught a bus in order to travel to another facility. We felt really bad about that. We realized that we had acted rather selfishly when we didn't stay with them until we knew everything was settled. Our concern that night had been getting sleep. Looking back, we see that we should have stayed with them until Ana had been born.

The day after Maria had little Ana, she was sent home from the hospital—to a noisy construction site lacking even the most basic amenities. The conditions were simply appalling, and I could not bear to think of such a young mother and a newborn being required to live amid the clamor of so many men with so little privacy and no one to help her recover from the strain of giving birth. I had the joy of bringing Maria to our house and helping her adjust to her new role as mother. I taught her about nursing, changing diapers, and bathing the baby. It was an unforgettable experience. Shortly after that Manoel and Maria accepted Christ as their Savior, and John and I had the privilege of discipling them in their spiritual growth.

We were heartened when Manoel and Maria decided to get married. They asked John to perform the ceremony. Both of them continued to grow in love for the Lord. In fact, one day Maria showed up at our door while I was teaching the children. She had saved up enough money to buy a bus ticket so she could come visit with me. Maria wanted me to read that week's Bible study lesson to her. Though she was illiterate and poor by the world's standards, she was rich in her hunger to learn more about God. John and I continue to enjoy a relationship with this couple and enjoy visits with them and their three daughters whenever we go to Brazil.

Elizabeth was another young lady who touched our lives that year. Only eighteen years old, she had had her first child at thirteen. She was married to a young man, Edilson, and they had a fifteen-month-old daughter, Ana Paula. Elizabeth had a fourth-grade education. When John first met this couple, they were living in a mud shack and Edilson was unemployed. From there they moved to an old farmhouse with one bed, a gas stove, and a few clothes. They didn't have any chairs or even a refrigerator. The old farmhouse had no running water—they collected water from a nearby stream. To have milk for Ana Paula and for themselves, they walked one mile to a local dairy farm.

Despite their worldly poverty, Edilson and Elizabeth were happy. Edilson had found a job since we had met them, and they were so grateful. They were thankful to have a roof over their heads and for the few things they had. They were thankful for little Ana Paula and the good health they all enjoyed. That spring John took them a Bible, and they were anxious to learn more about Jesus. We do not know the "end" of this story, but we are certain that God's Word never goes out in vain, and we feel privileged to have been able to share God's love and hope with them.

What about you?

*How much of your happiness is wrapped up in your posses-
sions? Put yourself in the place of the couples mentioned in this
narrative. What sort of attitude about life would you have if
you were in similar circumstances?*

*Who needs your help today? How can you go about meet-
ing their needs?*

ACTIONS SPEAK LOUDER
THAN WORDS

*Pure and lasting religion in the sight of God our Father
means that we must care for orphans and widows in their
troubles, and refuse to let the world corrupt us.*

— James 1:27

One point two million homeless children live in America. Two hundred thousand street children live in the alleyways of São Paulo, Brazil alone. Forty thousand orphans affected by AIDS live on the streets of Cambodia. Thirty-five million orphans affected by AIDS curl up to sleep on the streets of India each night. Twenty thousand Romanian street children face hunger and exposure every day. An estimated forty-three million African children will be orphaned by the AIDS virus by 2010.

Death. Poverty. War. Disease. Hunger. Cold. Abuse. Millions of children cry out around the globe naked, hungry, hurting, dying—alone. The following story describes one small way we strove to help. We haven't stopped asking the question, What more can we do? We hope you won't either. . .

After land was cleared and engineers and architects were hired to draw up plans, Lar WinShape, a foster home for Brazilian children, was completed after seven and a half months of work in Goias, Brazil, in 1991. The home was financed through the WinShape Foundation of Chick-fil-A, Incorporated of Atlanta, Georgia. The challenge of constructing a home thirty miles outside of Brasilia, the capital city, was great. Road systems and the communication infrastructure were not what you would expect in the States, so when I say challenge, I really mean it. But it was well worth it! The rewards of seeing the lives of children changed would more than compensate for any frustrations or obstacles of the construction process. We had chosen the foster parents, Sergio and Christina Stevenato, in the midst of building. Both of them spoke English, as well as Portuguese, and Christina even spoke German. The Stevenatos had a daughter of their own, Suzanna. Their faithfulness to the task proved beyond any shadow of a doubt that they were fully committed to loving and ministering to the children who would be in their care.

Why did we undertake such a huge project? There are over four million abandoned children in Brazil. We had firsthand experience of them—seeing them sleeping on the street and even picking through our garbage on a regular basis, trying to find food. The institutional orphanages were overburdened. For example, one had 120 boys with only one couple supervising them. Many had a ratio of one supervisor per fifty children. The foster home we had established, Lar WinShape, would accept only twelve children.

We hoped that limiting our numbers would allow the individual needs of each child to be met. We also wanted the children to grow up in an environment that modeled what a family was all about—not the sterile atmosphere of an institution. It was our desire that the family development concept would be a prototype for other foster homes to follow.

Initially, we had three children: Valmir, Luiz, and Michael. Years earlier, fifteen-year-old Valmir had been left at a drugstore by his father, who never returned to pick him up. He came to us on recommendation from the Baptist Children's Home in São Paulo. Luiz had been adopted at the age of three and then again at twelve; he was abandoned by his adoptive mother. After having been abandoned twice, he was fourteen when he came to Lar WinShape. Previously he had lived in the children's home in Sao Paulo for two years. Michael was only six when we met him. His mother had not wanted him and gave him to a couple to raise. The couple had taken in many unwanted children and had started a small orphanage with about twenty children by expanding their own home.

In June 1991, we had the joy of reuniting two sisters. The older sister had been living with a single woman in various locations in Brasilia. The other sister, Juliana, was living with her alcoholic father in a farm shack in the interior of the country. Juliana was only six years old. She stayed in our home for a week before going out to the Lar with her sister. During that week, she learned for the first time about running water and electricity. She made the cutest little giggle whenever she flipped on a light switch. Both girls accepted Christ as their Savior and grew splendidly under Sergio and Christina's love and guidance.

In the twelve years since the home opened, we have had the joy of touching the lives of twenty-five children. Though we prefer to keep the children long-term, there have been situations where some of them have had to be returned to extended family members, and a few children have even chosen to leave the home. Regardless of the time we have them, we know their lives can never be quite the same after living in a home where such genuine love is expressed to each of them.

Currently ten children live at the Lar. The oldest graduated from high school and is studying nutrition at the university in Brasilia. Over the years many of the children have become believers, and all are active in church, including Juliana, who teaches Sunday school to preschoolers. Our newest children, a brother and sister, were abandoned by their parents. Their parents locked them in the house and left them, never to return. We are delighted to have them at the Lar. Clearly, the needs are still great.

We often remind Sergio and Christina that while they know they are planting seeds of love and faith in each of these precious lives, they may never know the results or see the fruit as it develops and grows in the lives of the children. For the children who stay in touch, we have had the joy of watching them grow up, and the rewards have been priceless. Giving hands, feet, and action to love—isn't that what Christ calls us to do?

What about you?

Rather than writing, why not take a little time to research the statistics presented at the opening of this devotion? Unfortunately, you may find the numbers a bit higher when you read this than when I was writing. Whom will you tell? How will you get involved?

FOLLOWING HIM

[Jesus said] "My sheep recognize my voice;
I know them, and they follow me."

—*John 10:27*

How much do you know about sheep? If you want to fully understand the meaning of Jesus' words, you need to learn a bit about them. Many times Jesus refers to His followers as sheep. At first glance this might seem to be a neutral comparison—He might have chosen to call us cows or goats, right? But Jesus chose to call us sheep, and He did so with purpose.

Did you know that sheep are not known for their intelligence? If one sheep runs off a cliff, the rest of the flock is bound to follow. Sheep will eat frosty grass and die hours later from swollen intestines. They will limp around with a thorn in their hoof rather than trying to remove the noisome object or letting their shepherd help. Sheep will even try to force themselves into spaces that are too small to accommodate their bodies, making themselves vulnerable to attack. Without human intervention, sheep (unlike cows or goats) would not survive. One thing sheep are good at, though, is recognizing their shepherd, responding to his voice, and looking to him for food.

Like sheep, we often do foolish things. At times we put ourselves in danger or refuse to let others help us. The depth of our relationship with Jesus—the extent of our willingness to respond to His voice and our desire to be fed by Him—determines our well-being. That doesn't mean the Christian life is easy. Just as a sheep may cry out under the shepherd's shears or struggle and groan as the shepherd cleans and cares for its hooves, we too may experience discomfort as we let God direct our steps. We, however, can trust that He knows best.

On July 8, 1994, John received a call from Avery Willis, vice president for overseas operations at the International Mission Board in Richmond, Virginia. Avery asked if John would be interested in coming to Richmond to work as his assistant. My immediate reaction was not one of joy—in fact, my heart was in jeopardy of being completely hardened to the idea. If we were going to leave Brazil for the States, I certainly didn't want to have to go to Richmond. My family was in Georgia. But the Lord began working on me and encouraged me not to harden my heart against this possibility.

By the next day, I had surrendered myself to the Lord's will, but the struggle and transformation were just beginning. I had chosen to seek God's will, and now He was going to use that "permission" to change my heart and help me grow. John and I spent time praying over the decision together, and we decided not to share the news of Avery's request with our children until we felt we had an answer. We were surprised, then, about two weeks later when one of our church members, Irma Ceilde, prayed for us, saying that she was confident God would use us in Brazil—or even in the States.

The possibility of ending my missionary career in Brazil made me think again about my surrender to God concerning becoming an overseas missionary in the first place. Over ten years earlier He had enlarged my heart to seek His will and *go*—and we went. Now it seemed the time had come to enlarge my heart again as He pointed in a new direction. But when I had searched for guidance back then, I had felt a gnawing discontent, even though I thought I had finally achieved all I had ever dreamed of. I had lacked peace in the midst of my "happiness." Now, as God was speaking to my heart again, I struggled with the knowledge that I was peaceful and content serving and raising my family in Brazil. Why leave?

Though I felt apprehensive about the idea of returning to the States and grieved over the thought of leaving behind so many precious people in Brazil, I asked God to give me strength and assurance and to prepare the hearts of all those I loved if the change indeed was going to occur. I prayed especially hard for my children as they would have to face yet another transition. Saying goodbye is deeply painful. The lives of missionaries and their children are ever tempered by that ache. I could not deny the hurt, but I knew God's grace would be sufficient.

By July 26, John and I had reached a tentative decision. We felt that the Lord might truly be calling us back to the States, but we wanted to hear again from Avery. In His wisdom, God saw fit to have us wait—for a month! Avery's travel schedule was extremely busy, and we were not able to communicate with him during those four weeks. Once again, God used this time as an opportunity to hone our waiting skills and build in us an even more enduring faith. Over that month, I found myself concerned about what would happen with the children's schooling, anxious at times to hear the phone ring, and frustrated with God's silence. What a wonderful time of learning! I can assure you, however, that I didn't say that at the time.

By the end of August I asked the Lord to help me make the most of my days. I did not want to spend them idly speculating about what tomorrow would bring or waiting for word from Avery. I recognized that many opportunities were coming my way each day, and if I didn't act on them, they would be gone forever. I needed to stop focusing on what *could* happen and throw my energies into caring for my family and being sensitive to the people around me who were desperate to know the Lord. I confessed my weaknesses to God and asked Him to help me serve Him fully while I waited.

Finally, on August 26, after having heard from Avery and taking care of various details, John and I enjoyed a dinner out together as we celebrated our decision. The next morning, everything was peaceful. All of the waiting had brought on a lot of stress, but that pressure forced John and me to depend wholly on God rather than on ourselves. I knew that our resignation as missionaries was just around the corner and that my role and location would soon change, but I had confidence that the Lord had forever changed my view of missions and I would never see the world the same way again.

Over those next two weeks, we shared our decision with our children and our families in the States. Our families in America were thrilled to hear of John's promotion and happy that we would be closer. The children listened to the news with mixed emotions. I knew this would be a difficult time for all of us as we said goodbye to our home in Brazil. Going back to America would not be easy, even though it was our "home" culture. Our hearts had grown deeply attached to our friends and "family" in Brazil. In fact, I read somewhere that we should expect our return to the States to be an even more difficult adjustment than our transition to Brazil. Though we were supposed to feel comfortable and happy to be "home" in the States, the grief and longing for Brazil would result in our feeling torn. We anticipated much pain and joy as the result of this new direction God was leading us, and indeed we experienced both in large measures.

Hard times would follow, but we never had to go through them alone. We were confident that we were following God's voice, and He was faithful to lead and comfort us. After all, it is in those moments when the Shepherd is comforting His sheep that He must hold them the closest.

What about you?

Share a time in your life when you faced an important de-cision. What feelings did you experience? Where did you find comfort in the midst of the uncertainty?

CHANGES

But to all who believed him and accepted him, he
gave the right to become children of God.
—John 1:12

Long ago, even before he made the world, God loved us and
chose us in Christ to be holy and without fault in his eyes.
His unchanging plan has always been to adopt us into his
own family by bringing us to himself through Jesus Christ.
And this gave him great pleasure.
—Ephesians 1: 4-5

If we could live our lives in the full embrace of the preceding verses, what a difference it would make! So often we experience heartache when our circumstances change or when a familiar identity, one that we have wrapped ourselves in and called ourselves by for some time, is suddenly rendered out of date. It is my prayer for you, and for me—for this is a lesson we are constantly reviewing throughout our lives—that your identity will be rooted in the promise that you are fully acceptable and pleasing to God as a result of your belief in and confession of Jesus Christ as your Lord and Savior. You are His child! Let that truth define you; let it be your anchor, for all other things are likely to change.

In 1995, our family set out for Richmond, Virginia, so that John could transition from the mission field to his position with the home office of the International Mission Board. We had spent several enjoyable months near my family in Georgia after our return from Brazil, but now that was coming to an end. Leaving Georgia for Virginia was not easy; in fact, it was almost as difficult as leaving Georgia for Brazil. Virginia seemed like a foreign place to me. After all, I had no friends or family in Richmond, and the surroundings were simply unfamiliar.

After a couple of weeks of settling into our new home and enrolling the children in school, John and I went to get my Virginia driver's license. When I arrived at the Department of Motor Vehicles (DMV), the lady behind the counter asked for my Georgia license, then directed me to the photographer. I had my picture taken and after a few moments, my number was called and I went up to the counter to collect my new ID. Little did I know that I would be losing my old identification—literally and figuratively!

As I was about to turn away from the counter with my Virginia license in hand, I turned back, remembering she still had my Georgia license. I said to the woman,

"May I have my Georgia license back to keep?" She replied that I could not have it back—that it was not possible for me to have more than one license. I began pleading, "But I've had a Georgia license all my life, and even when we were overseas, I used that license along with my international one." This did not convince her. She maintained that it was illegal to hold two licenses. I was greatly disturbed.

Whenever we had returned to the States from Brazil, I renewed my Georgia license. It had become very important to me, and I wanted to at least hang on to it. That license had been the link to my identity as a native Georgian—no matter where I was in the world, Georgia was home and I had proof! But not any more. As I looked down at that Virginia license, my emotions began to swell.

I was trying to adjust to the fact that I was living in the state of Virginia, which I didn't know anything about. Living in Richmond where I had no friends, no church home, or familiar Georgian culture. Many people didn't even understand me and often asked, "Where are you from?" in response to my Georgia accent. Yes, I was finding even the language in Virginia was different! The fact that the DMV wouldn't give me my Georgia license back really frustrated me.

John came up to the counter and got me, and we headed out the door together. I was complaining to him and started crying. I sobbed, "This is just not fair!

Everything I've ever been a part of has been knocked out from under me. I don't have a church home anymore, I don't have any friends . . ." I went on and on down my list of woes. I felt so alone and isolated in this new city. The adjustment for me was tremendous.

We got in the car and John tried to comfort me. Not getting my license back was just the last straw, and he could see that. It was the last thing that I really thought was mine, and I didn't have it anymore. I was almost angry at God because I felt like He had taken everything away from me that made me, *me*. John reminded me, "You know the most precious thing that you have, that no one can ever take away, is your relationship with God. You will always be His child, and it doesn't matter where you go in the world, you will never lose that. You need to be grateful for that fact."

His words soothed me and helped me realize how valuable my identity in Christ and my relationship with God were. This realization made other things seem less important. Here I was, trying to adjust to a place that I didn't feel comfortable in—I felt like such a stranger in Richmond. It was comforting to be reminded that I was God's child and that He would never leave me nor forsake me. My identity was securely anchored in Him. To Him, I would always belong.

What about you?

Think of three major changes you have dealt with in your life. Describe how you felt when you knew things were about to change, how you felt in the midst of the changes, and what you learned as a result of having experienced them.

CAUSE FOR JOY

Listen to your father, who gave you life, and don't despise
your mother's experience when she is old. Get the truth
and don't ever sell it; also get wisdom, discipline, and
discernment. The father of godly children has cause
for joy. What a pleasure it is to have wise children. So give
your parents joy! May she who gave you birth be happy.
—Proverbs 23:22-25

My dream as a girl was to be a mother. In fact, I even prayed, asking Jesus to put off the Second Coming until I could have the joy of becoming a wife and mother! The time I spent with my children during our years in Brazil as their home-school teacher, moments of reading and talking with them, occasions spent watching them play an instrument or give their all in a sporting event—each of these is precious to me. I wouldn't trade those times for anything. I say unreservedly that I have great kids. I don't mean to imply that they haven't made mistakes or that we've never had to discipline them, but I would put them up against any other four children in the world and still claim them with the utmost pride as my own dear children. On May 18, 2002, my husband and I experienced a highlight in our parenting career: we gave our eldest daughter, Joy, in marriage to Trent Wilbanks, son of Mike and Susan Wilbanks of Ridgeland, Mississippi.

One Tuesday afternoon in January 1999, Joy called from her dorm room at Mississippi College to say, "Mother, remember the guy I told you I met at the ice cream place on Saturday? Well, tonight we're going out on a date to the movies." I immediately detected an unusual tone in her voice that left me wondering, *Could this be the one?* The young man's name was Trent Wilbanks. Joy and Trent had enjoyed quite a few dates together when I received an e-mail from him one day. I thought it was pretty brave and wise of Trent at the time. He wrote:

Hey! I'm Trent Wilbanks. I've wanted to e-mail you for a while . . . I just wanted to have some kind of contact with you since Joy and I are dating, and you don't have a clue who I am! I've got a lot of respect for your daughter and am impressed with the way y'all have raised her to love the Lord. She's a definite blessing.

Joy sure is excited about seeing y'all this weekend! She talks about you a good little bit! Oh yeah, and Mrs. White, that recipe for the dessert that you gave Joy the other night was really good! I guess I'd better go get some sleep! I just wanted to "introduce" myself since we can't exactly drop by to say hi!

After getting to know Trent through Joy's many phone calls and through meeting him personally, I was anxious to meet his parents, who had obviously invested much time and love into their son's life and raised him to be a godly man. Trent's sincere love for the Lord and his easygoing demeanor were well suited to our Joy.

Susan Wilbanks and I first met in the hallway at a children's music conference. We laughed together when she shared that she had been praying for Trent to find a special friend to bond with and hold him accountable for his spiritual growth, but she never imagined that special friend would be a girl named Joy! Trent and Joy were both freshmen that year at Mississippi College. Like Susan, John and I had been praying for Joy to form special lifelong friendships that would encourage her faith and provide loving fellowship. All of those prayers were answered.

Trent and Joy's relationship continued to deepen and grow. In the spring of their junior year, Trent approached John and me, requesting permission to ask Joy to be his wife. We gave him our blessings, and he enlisted our help in proposing to our daughter in a creative and romantic way. The next day he took Joy on quite an adventure, and when they returned to the cabin our family was vacationing in, a ring adorned Joy's finger, and their faces glowed with excitement.

A little more than a year later, May 18, 2002, just a week after they graduated from Mississippi College,

Trent and Joy were united in marriage. It was a great time of celebration. It was such an answer to prayer for Joy to find someone like Trent. We were grateful that God had guided her life and kept her pure and searching for a godly man.

During that ceremony, John and I took a few moments to share some thoughts with all of those gathered. I'd like to share a bit of what I said here:

Tonight we all have the privilege of witnessing the incredible fulfillment of God's written word: "The prayer of a righteous man availeth much." Go with me back a few years when Joy was just becoming a teenager, and allow me to share with you my written prayer for a complete stranger, who I now know today to be Trent Wilbanks.

Lord, I pray for the young man who will one day marry my daughter, Joy. I pray that he will be a man who loves You with his whole heart and that he will love You more than he loves her. Protect his heart and mind, Lord, so that he will be able to love her with a love that's pure. Remind him to pursue You above all else. Place around him Christians who will not just point the way but be the example he needs. I don't know who this man is, Lord, but help him this day to respect the girls in his life. Help him not to be overcome by passion for another but to keep himself pure for his wedding night with our little girl. Bring him into our daughter's life at the right time, and may their marriage be a light to all who see them together for many, many years.

John and I want to thank each one of you for the contribution you have made to the lives of Joy and Trent. We know we speak for Mike and Susan when we say that as parents, we have prayed earnestly to God for our children to grow up and follow Him.

I know that God is going to tremendously bless Trent and Joy's life together and that because He brought them together, He will keep them together. Trent and Joy celebrated their first anniversary in May 2003. They've had a wonderful year and continue to grow their love, keeping God's love as the rock of their relationship. John and I consider it a great privilege to faithfully pray for them both. Indeed, they have given us reason for joy.

What about you?

If you are a parent, share a moment when your child—or each of your children—gave you great joy. It could be the child's first smile, that precious time when you went into your child's room and watched him or her sleeping so peacefully, or your child's wedding day. Take some time to write about those moments. Your children will delight in reading your memories.

If you don't have children, describe a time when your brothers or sisters, parents, spouse, or another relative or friend gave you cause for great joy. Reflect on how richly other people bless your life.

IMPACT 360

Know.

What does God have to say about the tough issues facing our culture? Get answers through interactive learning with guest professors and staff who help you develop a Biblical world and life view.

Be.

Who has God made you to be? Discover your strengths and gifts and how they can be used for God's kingdom. Receive leadership training and learn how servant leadership can make a lasting impact.

Live.

Ready to live out your faith? Students participate in a month-long international mission trip, working alongside missionaries in another country.

"IMPACT 360 has dramatically transformed the way I look at the world so that I can best respond to whatever plans God has prepared for me."

— George Argyris, IMPACT 360 (Alumnus–Murrieta, California)

Here's the 411!

- 9-Month Program (September–May) Just Outside Metro Atlanta, GA
- 15 Hours of College Credit from Union University
- 4-week International Experience
- Leadership Training Through Chick-fil-A University
- Internationally-Renowned Guest Professors and Speakers

www.impact360.net